Sil

by
David Runcorn
Sometime Chaplain of Lee Abbey, North Devon
Assistant Curate, St. Stephen's Church, West Ealing

GROVE BOOKS LIMITED
Bramcote   Nottingham   NG9 3DS

CONTENTS

DEDICATION

With love and thanks to the Lee Abbey Community in the gift of 'Life Together'.

Special thanks to Lindsay Dinan for the cover design and to Alyse Newby for her typing skills.

First Edition February 1986
Second Edition July 1989
ISSN 0262-799X
ISBN 1 85174 113 5

INTRODUCTION

'Somewhere in the tunnel between Victoria and Green Park, the tube train stops for no apparent reason. The noise of the engine dies abruptly and a harsh stillness descends on the passengers. Conversation that was being shouted moments before now becomes subdued and self-conscious. The silence is uncomfortable. We avoid each other's eyes. There is a need to be doing something. We cough, blow our noses, re-read the newspaper—anything to fill the emptiness of the moment. At last the train comes to life again. Noise fills the world and the relief is almost tangible.'

Do you know the feeling? We have an awkward relationship with silence. It attracts us and repels us. We protest loudly that 'all I want is some peace and quiet', but, given an unexpected hour of space, we have to go looking for something to fill it. Even in our churches we speak more about silence than we allow it. How often the invitation to be 'quiet before the Lord' takes longer than the silence that follows!

We may be coming to a book like this with the feeling that we are approaching something new. We may even feel that there is something about silence that 'is not natural'. It may help us to realize that silence is much more a part of our noisy world than we are generally aware. It surrounds and influences all aspects of our lives—however profound or ordinary.

We have all had times on holiday when a bend in the road surprises us with some quite spectacular scenery. All conversation stops. We gaze in silence. It is (literally) breathtaking.

Times of grief and tragedy can leave us silent and numb. At such times it is the silent company of friends that we appreciate most—not their words.

Silence can be quite unpredictable in its moods though. For example, I may enjoy a quiet evening by the fire, on my own and content to be so— thinking of little and doing nothing in particular. On another occasion such an evening would be agonizing. It might feel overwhelmingly lonely and the silence of the room becomes unbearable.

Lovers lapse into silences without knowing it—completely absorbed in each other's company. But for another relationship silence is a deadlock and an awful inability to communicate. Silence may express positive involvement, or passive (even negative) non-involvement. An angry silence is a withdrawal weapon in conflict. Some things, we say, are 'better left unsaid'. Police investigation can meet with a 'wall of silence' that is non-cooperation.

So what is this thing called silence that at either extreme of experience will complete our joys or confirm our dread? It speaks of solemn gratitude at the Cenotaph. It keeps those birthday secrets hidden until the day! It breaks the mind and will of the man in the solitary cell. It is the legendary choice of the British in the rush-hour train!

Perhaps the mistake we often make is to assume that silence is the possession of a particular mood or emotion. It is very easy, for example, for children only to understand silence as a rebuke (from parents) or a punishment (at school). But in all the varied encounters of our lives, of whatever the nature, silence is part of an inner response that invites us to *deepen* the moment. It expresses the need to 'take it in'. It may accompany feelings of joy or grief, excitement or despair, but its gift will be to allow the moment to 'sink in' and go deep. If we refuse the gift then we remain on the surface of it all.

All these 'accidental' or spontaneous brushes with silence are not enough. Spontaneity cannot be the foundation for mature spiritual growth any more than it can be for human relationships. If we are not to remain strangers to silence, we must choose what we seek—we must 'will' to be silent.

Having said all that, let me close this Introduction by sharing my first encounter with silence.

Some years ago I stayed at the Taizé community in France for a week.

The thousands of young people who pack Taizé each summer are encouraged to participate in the daily round of worship and to choose, from a variety of different themes, a group for daily Bible study and discussion.

Faced with crowds of strange people and feeling that I had really come for a holiday, I opted for the last one on the list—the 'pays de silence' (field of silence). I cannot claim any higher motivation than that!

Between the church and the sprawling camp sites, a small field was set apart with basic facilities for those who wished to spend time in silence. The day was unstructured with the exception of a short Bible reading each morning from one of the brothers and an optional 'talking time' over tea in the afternoon.

For all the impulsiveness of my initial choice I felt a growing enthusiasm for the idea. I wanted to have a go at 'being silent'. In the warm afternoon sunshine I sat down on the grass with my Bible and tried to still myself for God.

I found I could not. I was almost immediately overwhelmed by a torrent of random thoughts and feelings. Rather than feeling peaceful and closer to God, I was drowning in a turbulent flood of clamour within that made concentration quite impossible. I did not know such noise was in me! It was as if the act of being silent had lifted off the lid from all kinds of voices within that I did not know were there. They were powerful too. Prayer and reading was hopeless. I soon felt completely desolate and worn out by the struggle. It was all so unexpected.

For three days I could only wander restlessly, attending the worship and wondering if it was not a mistake to have ever tried. After four days I became dimly aware that the flood was slowing down. At last there were moments of genuine stillness in which I began, very chastened, to pray.

1. THE ROOTS OF SILENCE

'Silence is of various depths and fertility, like soil. Now it is a Sahara, where men perish of hunger and thirst, now a fertile bottom, or prairie, of the West.'

(Henry David Thoreau)

'Yahweh is first and foremost a God of the Wilderness.'

(Kenneth Leech)

We begin by looking at the place of silence in the scriptures.

If our culture struggles with silence for fear that it brings an 'absence', the Bible understands that silence is a wrestling with 'presence'. The presence of God. We have a tendency at this point to stay with familiar and comfortable texts of the subject—'Be still, and know that I am God!'. But silence is clearly more than just an aspect of the spiritual life. Kenneth Leech argues that in a profound sense the faith of God's people was born out of silence—the solitary, rugged silence of the wilderness.[1] It was here too that it had to grow and mature.

We are well accustomed to studying the *words* of the scriptures. We neglect the *silences*. This may seem a strange suggestion at first, but in fact communication and language actually depend as much on silence as on the words between. The ability of an actor or comedian to give power and humour to his lines comes out of his skill to use timing and silence. Someone once described language as a 'cord of silence', and the words are knots in it.

If there is a cord of silence linking the words of scripture it is found in the wilderness. We must learn to meditate on the silences of scripture if we are to enter into the life and faith behind the words.

To understand the spiritual roots of God's people then, we need to consider the influence of the desert in their living experience. It is those dry solitary wastes that provide the Hebrew people with their most vivid imagery in prayer and worship.

> 'O God, you are my God
> earnestly I seek you,
> my soul thirsts for you,
> my body longs for you,
> in a dry and weary land
> where there is no water.' (Ps. 63.1)

But more fundamentally, we must look at the possibility that this desert silence says something about God himself. It may be with silence rather than words that we will ever draw near the Eternal Presence. What marked out this Wilderness God of the Hebrews from other gods was that he could *not* be expressed. No art could express his likeness and no words could avoid falling short—and so mis-representing him. Any attempt to do so became an idol. The true God is inexpressible in the mystery of his holiness. He is, and dwells in, silence. As Henri Nouwen says 'silence alone shares something of God's infinity.'[2] So the place of meeting must be the desert of loving silence.

[1] *True God* (Sheldon, 1985) Chap. 5.
[2] *The Way of the Heart—Desert Spirituality and Contemporary Ministry* (DLT, 1981) p.33.

5

'One Word the Father spoke, which Word was his Son, and this Word he ever speaks in eternal silence and in silence it must be heard by the soul.'[1]

(St. John of the Cross)

In a study entitled 'The God of the Desert', Kenneth Leech suggests four characteristics of desert spirituality in the Bible that lie at the heart of a Christian understanding of prayer.[2] We will use these to explore the place of silence a little more.

Simplicity

The desert is a place where we are simplified and stripped of all non-essentials of life.

There is a scene in the film 'Lawrence of Arabia' when a man finds himself alone in the middle of the desert and begins a desperate journey to safety.

As the sun gets hotter he casts off piece after piece of his possessions and clothing (his former securities)—his gun, his ammunition belt, his knife, his cloak . . . a proud warrior mercilessly stripped to nothing. He finally collapses on the desert sands and lies there helplessly, waiting rescue or death.

So the desert is the place where God's people learn hard lessons of life and faith. It is a place to learn the real priorities and there are no margins for error. In the desert there is no room for luxuries and no respect for human status or strength. To contemplate the desert, then, is to understand the call to walk by faith in God alone. It is a place that simplifies us, down to our true selves, until we are ready to meet the God of life and death.

René Voillaume puts it like this:

'The desert—the real desert—bears in its physical reality the sign of isolation, not only from people and human life, but from any semblance of man's activity and presence. Being something that man cannot put to use, it likewise bears the sign of aridity, and consequently the subduing of all the senses, including both sight and hearing. It also bears the sign of poverty and austerity, and of most extreme simplicity. In short, it bears the sign of man's complete helplessness, as he can do nothing to subsist alone and by himself in the desert, and thus he discovers his weakness and the necessity of seeking help and strength in God.'[3]

So we cannot speak of the desert, as just a geographical reality for some people. It is, for all of us, a sign of the 'Way of the Heart'. We all need to create a 'poustinia' in the heart—a desert place of silence and prayer.[4] It is a place to which we must withdraw as Jesus did, to be renewed in the midst of a busy world.

But, however much this is something we long for—desire itself is not enough. We need a point of entry into the clutter and insecurity of our lives so that they can be simplified for prayer and God. 'One way to nurture

---

[1] *Maximus on Love* No. 21.
[2] *op. cit.,* Chap. 5
[3] Cited by Leech *op. cit.* p.154-5.
[4] Catherine de Hueck Doherty, *Poustinia* (Fount, 1977).

simplicity is through the discipline of silence. Society is dominated by the inane notion that action is the only reality. Please, for God's sake and your own, don't just do something, stand there! Come in and enjoy his presence.'[1] Sometimes the simplest solutions are the hardest.

Henri Nouwen was seeking just this when he went to spend seven months in a monastery. His journal of that time was published as *The Genesee Diary*. In the introduction he discusses what led him to 'stop'.

'I realized that I was caught in a web of strange paradoxes. While complaining about too many demands, I felt uneasy when none were made. While speaking about the burden of letter writing, an empty mailbox made me sad. While fretting about tiring lecture tours, I felt disappointed when there were no invitations. While speaking nostalgically about an empty desk, I feared the day in which that would come true. In short, while desiring to be alone I was frightened of being left alone. The more I became aware of these paradoxes, the more I started to see how much I had indeed fallen in love with my own compulsions and illusions, and how much I needed to step back and wonder—is there a quiet stream underneath the fluctuating affirmations and rejections of my little world? Is there a still point where my life is anchored from which I can reach out with hope and courage and confidence?'[2]

It is a testimony that also reminds us that, more than we care to admit, the secret is re-discovering our freedom to choose—and to say 'no'!

Struggle

For this simplifying to happen, the desert becomes a place of testing—and so of struggle. To enter the security of God's love we must first let go of our own securities. 'Much religious life is geared to safety, not to sanctity, for sanctity involves danger, involves launching out into the deep, facing the wilderness, the dark night and the perils of Babylon.'[3]

Desert faith is therefore faith 'on the move'. It is nomadic. Abraham is its father (Heb. 1.1, 8-10). But Jesus himself completes our understanding. As John writes, 'The Word became flesh and *pitched his tent* among us' (John 1.14 literally). For his life on earth he once said 'The Son of Man has nowhere to lay his head' (Luke 9.58).[4]

The struggle is not to settle down, giving up the journey too soon, accepting lesser securities and so making idols of them. 'We must take the feeling of being at home into exile. We must be rooted in the absence of a place.'[5] The struggle is experienced in different ways.

We know that as Abraham responded to the call to move out into the strange land a 'great and dreadful darkness came upon him' (Gen. 15.12).

[1] Richard Foster *Freedom of Simplicity* (Triangle, 1981) p.58.
[2] (Image Books, 1981) p.14.
[3] Leech, *op. cit.,* p.159.
[4] Of course the Incarnation itself was not temporary but eternal—the taking of manhood into God.
[5] Simone Weil, *Gravity and Grace* (Routledge and Kegan Paul), p.34.

SILENCE

We are not told what it cost Moses, the prince of Pharoah's court, to live in exile, tending sheep in the wilderness for forty years. But whatever his struggles were they changed his life. It was a servant of the Lord who returned to Egypt.

Then there is Jacob's struggle at Jabbok and the mystery of a God who comes in the silence and darkness of the night, wrestling a man into his new name and identity (Gen. 32.22-32). There are many others through the scriptures whose lives were formed and transformed by their struggles with faith in the wilderness. It was a testing that even the Son of God was not spared.

The wilderness has different moods. There are times when it bursts with promise, an absurd hope of fruitfulness and new life. There are times when its fearful voids speak of a terrifying absence and God-forsaken emptiness.

The feature of wilderness faith, however, is its willingness to accept the absence of God without protest. Consider the fury of Habakkuk;

'Why are you silent while the wicked swallow up those more righteous than themselves!' (Hab. 1.13)

There is a boldness to faith (and doubt) which makes our Western spiritual tradition seem very passive by comparison. But the boldness to question and search will lead us directly into the vulnerability and night of desert faith. We will know the darkness of our own fears and the perils of our weaknesses. But that very struggle makes possible a new exposure to God himself. And so it is that of Habakkuk's wrestling a new strength and vision is born, for God has spoken:

'God is in his holy Temple—let all the earth keep silence before him.' (Hab. 2.20)

When we speak of silence in this context we recognize that it is something much more than those times of stillness in our church worship. The idea of silence in public worship has found much more place in recent years but it needs to be carefully and imaginatively introduced. Just to suggest 'a time of silence' will leave many people feeling confused as to how to use it. It will feel stressful—rather like being told to hold your breath for a time!

It is a fact that, for many, the experience of entering into silence is one of frightening alienation and inner turmoil. Far from the enticing vision of being 'alone with the Alone', it feels like a dubious invitation to be submerged in personal chaos and darkness. The important thing to note is that in such an event it is not a failure of the person or the silence.

Christian prayer is more often marked by struggle than peace. The presence of blissful feelings when I am silent does not mean that I am actually in God's presence. But if we are to encourage each other in the desert of silence we need to be growing in the maturity of our love and care of one another in the dryness or the night of faith. Someone once said that 'prayer and love are really learned in the hour when prayer becomes impossible.' Struggle is the fruit of faithfulness in the desert—not the failure of it.

We might well find that once we consent to seeking silence, it has a way of turning the tables and searching us! It is the work of the Holy Spirit to search all things (1 Cor. 2.10).

There is a chapel in a monastery to which I used to go for retreats where I knew that if I went to pray I would have to submit to the disturbing sensation of being spiritually 'undressed'. That is the only way I can describe it. The Quakers speak of a 'sifting silence' and I imagine that is what they mean.

Waiting

Some years ago I travelled across the Nubian desert of Northern Sudan and down the Nile to Cairo. It was a journey packed with vivid impressions but I remember it clearly for the amount of waiting that was involved.

Whatever level of life or organization, nothing hurried in the desert. And nothing should be hurried, it seems. Waiting was not an interruption to a man's journey. It was an essential part of the journey itself.

In our Western culture we have no positive use for waiting. Much technology and expense goes into reducing the waiting in our lives. It is an intrusion, a frustration, whether it be at the bus stop or by the letter box. It interrupts our timetables and delays our lives.[1]

But our God is the God of the desert. He is the 'Three mile an hour God'. He *walks* with his people.

Perhaps Elijah best expresses the dangers in our lifestyle. He too had lost the 'stature of waiting.' He learned the hard way that there was nothing to sustain him between noisy mountain tops of his ministry and the bitter deserts of his own exhaustion. He has to make a journey—from the mountain of his own activities, through the desert of his own emptiness, to Horeb, the mountain of God (1 Kings 18 and 19). There he waits in a cave as all the whirlwind, fire and vigour of his ministry passes before him and God is not in it. But there, behind it all, barely discernible—a 'small thin silence'.[2] It is the silence of God. Elijah has returned to the roots of his faith.

There is frustration that surfaces among Christians when 'silence' is mentioned once too often. Surely God is not silent? He has revealed himself and spoken. We have something to share and proclaim!

Zechariah must have felt this frustration acutely. He illustrates well the apparent contradiction of Christian silence. Here is an old man who knows the pain and frustration of waiting, for all his life he had longed and prayed for a child. Now, in old age, an angel appears and gives him an astonishing message of prophecy—and immediately strikes him dumb for his hesitation in receiving it! The Word of the Lord is locked up within him in silence. He is completely alone with the message all the world has been waiting to hear.

We do not know what those months meant to him, but like Elizabeth and Mary he was confined with the Word of Life. But when signs are made

[1] See W. H. Vanstone, *The Stature of Waiting* (DLT, 1982).
[2] The traditional 'still small voice' is not the most helpful reading.

to him to resolve the controversy over the name of his son, his response (in the Greek) is emphatic—'John *is* his name!' (Luke 2.63). There is fire in those bones! When his tongue is loosed he utters the song that Christian worship has been using ever since. Out of silence has emerged a prophet.

This capacity for taking in what God is saying or doing and 'waiting upon it' is vital. It is a quality that Luke found in Mary (Luke 2.18-19). We are also familiar with it in the rhythm of withdrawal and activity that Jesus lived by and impressed upon his disciples (Luke 5.16). Even after spectacular miracles of healing, Jesus is found urging people to silence about what has happened.[1] Theologians usually step in with an explanation at this point, but the intention may be quite practical: 'Where there was a danger of all deeper impressions being scattered and lost through the garrulous repetition of the outward circumstances of the healing, there silence was enjoined, that so there might be an inward brooding over the gracious and wondrous dealings of the Lord.'[2]

There is a time to speak and a time to be silent. We have to learn to resist the pressure to live on the surface of an experience or encounter. We must still ourselves and take it in. This is the fullest understanding of what it means to listen. So the desert of silence becomes a place of loving, attentive vigilance to the will of God and of reverent longing for his Word:

> 'I will lift my eyes to you,
> to you whose throne is in heaven.
> As the eyes of slaves look
> to the hand of their master,
> as the eyes of a maid
> look to the hand of her mistress,
> so our eyes look to the Lord our God.' (Ps. 123.1-3)

Adoration
Lest it be thought that faith in the desert must be one of grim struggle and endurance we finally recognize it as a place of worship and hope. For the promise of God's coming salvation is given, not to the cities and the rich places of human achievement, but to the wilderness and waste places. It is the desert that waits in hope for the salvation of our God:

> 'The desert and the parched land will be glad.
> The wilderness will rejoice and blossom.
> Like a crocus it will burst into bloom.
> It will rejoice greatly and shout for joy.
> The glory of Lebanon will be given to it
> and the splendour of Carmel and Sharon.
> They will see the glory of the Lord
> the splendour of our God . . .' (Is.35.1-3)

But the desert calls us to something fuller and richer still. It calls us to a vision of God—to adoration. Adoration begins when we are captivated by the living God—not for what he does or promises—but just *for who he is.*

[1] cf. Luke 8.27.30, Luke 8.54-56, Luke 9.35-36.
[2] Archbishop Trench, *Notes on the Miracles,* commenting on Mk. 5.19.

When we contemplate the solitary hours that Jesus spent in prayer in the hill

'Where Jesus knelt to share with thee
the silence of eternity,
interpreted by love.'

or read of the awesome outpouring of praise in the heavens (in Revelation)

'Holy, holy, holy is the Lord God Almighty
Who was, and is, and is to come.'

this is surely what we are drawing near?

There is much worship that stops short of adoration. In doing so it remains on the level of appreciation or another way of offering thanks to God. But adoration is not appreciation but *abandonment*—abandonment before the wonder and beauty of God in all his glory.

I once spent three months working on a Kibbutz in the Negev desert of Israel. I used to spend all my spare time wandering the sun-baked hills and arid plains around the settlement. But it was the experience of walking at night I remember most. There would be no-one else for miles—the simplicity and solitude were something spell-binding. There were moments of deep intensity as I seemed to feel the ancient strength of the wilderness rising to meet the sparkling infinity of the silent heavens. I would be completely lost in it. Although I could not understand what moved me, I knew that I deeply belonged in the mystery of it all. Time and again under those stars I stood breathless as the night, my whole being alive with wonder and awe.

Adoration of God must be something like that. It is being completely captivated by Love. It is knowing ourselves drawn in to the eternal life and love of the Trinity—'that they may be in *us*,' in the words of Jesus' prayer to the Father (John 17.21).

2. SILENCE AND THE 'LEAPING WORD'[1]

'You can listen to silence, Reuven, I've begun to realize that you can listen to silence and learn from it. It has a quality and dimension all of its own. It talks to me sometimes. I can feel myself alive in it. It talks. And I can hear it.'

(Chaim Potok, *The Chosen*)

'Many people ask me to speak,
no one asks me for silence,'

(Henri Nouwen)

We can now begin to explore what an understanding and experience of silence might contribute to our own living and praying. The possibilities are very diverse but we will try to consider a variety of them.

(a) Silence as a Way of Life

A dietician once described fasting as 'the punctuation marks in my relationship with food.' That may be a helpful way of expressing the relationship of silence to lifestyle. There must be punctuation in the script of our lives, giving it its flow, its pauses, its varieties of expression. It brings a subtlety and depth to it all.

In our Introduction we spoke of the 'spontaneous' moments when we encounter silence. They are, perhaps, the exclamation marks. But life needs the discipline of regular punctuation—its moments to pause, to catch breath, to reflect, or just to lie fallow for a time.

These will be the times we get back in touch with our deeper selves. Times we can, with loving suspicion, review the demands and priorities we have laid upon our lives. This is traditionally called a 'rule of life' and 'Finding a Personal Rule of Life'[2] has been a help to many who have felt the need for more disciplined punctuation of their lifestyle.

It is the 'full stops' that are the most difficult perhaps. The points at which we decide to halt completely—to sit still and be silent. It may be for an hour, a day, or a longer time away somewhere. But it is not surprising to find that one of our first reactions on entering silence is that we get angry. There may be no apparent reason for it. It is part of the struggle to 'let go'. We are stepping out of all that gives us a sense of worth and security. Silence is an unknown and unfamiliar territory. We are not in control any more. The 'eternal silence of the infinite spaces terrifies me', said Pascal. Silence itself is an encounter with infinity. That is why we feel so powerless, so empty and unable to do anything. It is very threatening.

At such times we must stay in the struggle and allow the Holy Spirit, in the silence, to ease our grip on the controls and yield them afresh to God.

The silence also assaults our notion of *usefulness*. What is the point of silence? What is the use of it? None at all on the face of it. But our assumptions about worth and usefulness need challenging themselves. Our culture still measures worth by activity and achievement. It is an approach to society that profoundly devalues the most vulnerable in our

---

[1] 'All things were lying in quiet and silence, and night in her swift course was half spent, when the Almighty Word leapt from thy Royal throne in heaven . . .' (Wisdom of Solomon 18.14). Though belonging to a different context, traditionally used as a Christian antiphon.

[2] This is the title of Grove Spirituality Series no. 8 by Harold Miller (1983).

midst—not least the unemployed and the elderly at this time. Silence must profoundly disturb us in these false estimates of ourselves. It calls us to confess them, to die to them, and so to enter new life in Christ.

(b) Solitude and Community

Dietrich Bonhoeffer always taught that the ability to live in community requires the freedom to be alone. Unless we have that freedom, then we will always be using our life together to hide from what we cannot face in ourselves. It is in solitude that we seek our place in community and it is in community that we find strength for our solitude.[1]

It is sad that our culture, and often our churches, make us feel that spending time alone is selfish. We feel guilty for wanting to 'go off on our own'. Our commitment to each other is measured by our active involvement together. This is quite false. As one writer expressed it:

> 'we do not go into the desert to escape people but to learn how to find them; we do not leave them in order to have nothing to do with them, but to find out the way to do them the most good. But this is only a secondary end. The end that includes all the others is the love of God.'[2]

Without these roots in solitude and silence, our life together will all too easily be sustained by an incessant whirl of activity. Our activity will be all that we have to affirm us. The simple truth is that Christian fellowship sustained in such a way may be exciting for a time but it cannot truly liberate and give life. It can only enslave us to the round of it all. We will get stuck and exhausted. Alan Ecclestone suggests that in all this what we need is:

> '... a solvent of those devices and rigid forms which are imposed upon life—and silence is such a solvent. There is a kind of silence in which the hard thick shell which normally covers and protects us, the thick shell of fiction and prejudice and readymade phrases which separate man from man, begins to crack and open. The silence that liberates is among the great needs of our time.'[3]

(c) Silence and Words

Silence is not an abandoning of words. Silence expresses our reverence for words and reminds us to respect their truth and power.

After some weeks of sharing the silent life of a Cistercian monastery, Henri Nouwen was aware of a growing sense of responsibility for the words he used. After one conversation he experienced remorse. 'I felt as if I had touched something that should not be touched, as if I had distorted something simply by talking about it, as if I had tried to grasp a dew drop.'[4] We have a responsibility for the words we use. They are not to be wasted or misused. Nouwen's experience of silence led him to repent of his careless wordiness.

[1] *Life Together* (SCM, 1954) pp.77-8.
[2] Thomas Merton, *Thoughts in Solitude* (Burns and Oates, 1958) p.22.
[3] *A Staircase for Silence* (DLT, 1977) p.42.
[4] *op. cit.* p.134.

13

Not only does Jesus make clear that we will not be any more heard for pil-
ing up words to God (Matt. 6.7), but James sternly warns us that:
>'the tongue is a small part . . . but it makes great boasts . . . the tongue
>is also a fire . . . it corrupts the whole person . . . out of the same mouth
>comes praising and cursing . . . this should not be' (Jas. 3.5ff.).

But that is the way it is. He is not exaggerating. The same tongue we use to
pray and to worship God is compulsively at work at other times to
manipulate, to self-justify, to flatter for influence—a ceaseless torrent of
communication devoted to the maintenance and control of our own little
worlds. 'Silence is one of the deepest disciplines of the Spirit simply
because it puts a stopper on all that!'[1]

St. Ignatius taught that our silence can point people to God more than our
words. So he expects this quality most of all in church leaders:
>'A bishop should be particularly revered when he is silent. The silence
>of a bishop bears witness to the reality of God, both in the mystery of
>his divine silence and in the silence of his passion. The church is the
>place where all things pass over into reality by being plunged into the
>hidden reality of God, so that the outer and inner become one, the
>word and silence are reunited.'[2]

Silence deepens communication. I remember the comment of a person
who came to a retreat at Lee Abbey and was dismayed to discover that half
of each day would be spent in silence. But at the end of the week she said,
'you know, I think I know all these people better now than if I had spent the
week talking to them!' Once we have got over our awkwardness, silence
seems to bring a new sensitivity to our relationships. In a quiet way a new
society can emerge out of silence in which the eloquent are humbled and
the tongue-tied exalted. Then we may find God speaking through people
who have never had the courage to contribute before. We will learn to
'honour those parts which appear weaker' (1 Cor. 12.21-26).
>'It is in solitude that I find the gentleness with which I am to truly love
>my brothers. The more solitary I am the more affection I have for
>them. It is pure affection and filled with reverence for the solitude of
>others. Solitude and silence teach me to love my brothers for what
>they are, not for what they say.'[3]

(d) 'The Language of the Mad'
Christianity is not the only faith to speak of silence. Far from it. It is a quality
of attentiveness and expression that other cultures and religions have
often understood much better. African culture, for example, understands
the power and meaning of 'presence' between people, where Western
culture would be uncomfortable without words.

We have seen silence used as both a protest and a political weapon in this
century. Louis Fischer perceptively observes of Mahatma Gandhi:
>'. . . sometimes, if he was too tired or the crowd too noisy, he would sit
>on the platform in silence until the audience, which often numbered
>two hundred thousand, became quiet. He then continued to sit in
>silence, and the men and women sat in silence, and he touched his
>palms together to bless them, and smiled and departed. This was

[1] Foster op. cit. p.58.
[2] cited by Simon Tugwell, Ways of Imperfection (SCM, 1984) p.4.
[3] Thomas Merton, Sign of Jonas (Sheldon, 1976) p.268.

communication without words, and the mass silence was an exercise in self-control and self-searching, a step therefore towards self-rule.'[1]

A Christian understanding of silence will also have this note of protest to it. The silent spirit of the Quaker movement has kept it in the forefront of Christian concern on social and political issues.

We are not just concerned for the words we speak. We have a responsibility for the words by which the world is living—a concern for truth wherever it is expressed. In his novel *Proteus,* Morris West writes this conversation between the Russian Ambassador and a personal friend:

'—what is the thing you are most afraid of?'
'—politically or personally?'
'—both'
'—it is a thing which has happened already, whose human consequences are already upon us. We have so debased human language that it is impossible to believe any longer what we hear or read. I tell you "yes", the echo answers "no". We state one position and negotiate another. You talk "food", I hear "bombs". We have created a language of the mad. You show on television bodies broken in a railway accident. The next instant some impossibly beautiful wench is demonstrating how to make floors shine like glass. The illusion is complete. There are no bodies. There could never be blood on so bright a surface.'[2]

We have created a language of the mad. It was with this kind of discernment that Merton would speak of the priority of prayer as 'the unmasking of illusion'. It is to be the place of truth. There is a striking parallel in the comments of a man from Beirut, about prayer for the Middle East:

'the difficulty [re. the Middle East] . . . is that words have lost their meaning. For instance, if you mention hope, you might as well be talking about despair for all the effect it has on people. Therefore I would talk mostly of waiting upon God and quietly searching for his presence. Real prayer is offering what you can see and grasping what is happening, however painful and beastly it is, and waiting on God with it, almost as though you have it in your hands'.[3]

(e) Silence and Suffering

One of the most unforgettable impressions from watching the film of the Ethiopian famine and the refugee camps was the silence of the suffering there. Silence is a friend of suffering. With his insight from the Jewish Hasidic tradition Chaim Potok wrote *The Chosen.* In the story a boy is brought up in silence by his father, a Hasid Rabbi. He later begins to speak of the experience to a friend:

'You can listen to silence, Reuven . . . you have to want to listen to it. It has a strange and beautiful texture. It doesn't always talk. Sometimes—sometimes it cries, and you hear the pain of the world in it. It hurts to listen then. But you have to'.[4]

The difficulty of praying for 'the world' is that its pains and conflicts feel so vast and complex. We are helpless to put prayer into words and generally feel as if the failure to 'say it right' is a failure in the prayer itself. That is not so.

[1] *The Life of Mahatma Gandhi* (Granada, 1982) p.311.
[2] (Collins, 1979) p.184.
[3] Alan Amos interviewed in *Grassroots* magazine (February 1983).
[4] (Penguin 1970) p.259.

When we seek to pray into the pain of the world we are drawing near to the cross. We are seeking to join with the intercession of Christ. That is what Christian prayer is all about. The striking fact is that the nearer Jesus got to his cross the less he spoke. There is, as one person put it, 'an enormous and dreadful solitude' around those events. He fulfils Isaiah's vision of the servant who suffers in silence. 'He opened not his mouth' (Is. 53.7). It is a participation in suffering that words cannot express. It is a suffering completely beyond words as he willingly descended into that hell of man's sin and estrangement.

A faith centred on the cross will certainly feel tongue-tied with its burden at times. We must learn the prayer of silence. There is no other way.

Our Western Christian understanding of prayer and intercession is almost completely verbal. This inhibits us. We need alternative ways of expressing our prayer in a suffering world. One helpful idea has been used at Lee Abbey on occasions. The leader invites the congregation to express intercesssion by using three simple movements of the hands.

—hands cupped (as if holding something in them)—we are invited to give thanks for all that God has given us over the past week (a silence is kept).

—hands reaching out (as if to show God a suffering world)—we are invited to pray for the world in its suffering and pain (there may be particular needs—a silence is kept).

—hands reaching up (as in longing and welcome)—we express our hope in God for the world he comes to save (a silence is kept).

The combination of silent prayer and simple movement has led some people to a quite new involvement in intercessory prayer.

(f) Silent for God

While working in a parish in London I was, for a time, a member of a weekly home group. We met each Wednesday evening after a full working day, to plunge into coffee, fellowship and Bible study. As some began to find this simply adding to the activity of the day rather than providing a refreshment from it, we agreed to begin our evenings together with ten minutes of silence. One person would read a passage of Scripture and then we were still. During the weeks we met in that way we found that our evenings became focused on God in a new way. This was not dramatic and some of us felt it more than others, but we had (in Quaker language) 'centred down'. We were capable of a new responsiveness to God and to each other. We also found that God would speak during the silence—a guiding word, a picture, or a verse of Scripture.

God is the goal of our silence. It is God himself we are seeking and we are silent for him. It is very easy to use prayer to invite God into our presence and activity. In silence we seek to enter God's presence and attend to his activity. It is also a temptation to seek silence for itself—for the feelings we might have of love and peace. As soon as we do this we are no longer seeking God. Christian silence is the prayer that seeks the living God out of the heart of this broken world.[1]

[1] For further illustration of this, see the quotation from Thomas Merton on p.21.

3. CREATIVE SILENCE

Sarah: I live in a place you can't enter. It's out of reach.

James: Out of reach? That sounds romantic.

Sarah: Deafness isn't the opposite of hearing, as you think. It's a silence full of sound.

James: It's a silence full of sound?

Sarah: The sound of spring breaking up through the death of winter.

(from *Children of a Lesser God*)[1]

Our churches are very diligent in urging us to pray *more*. Most of us feel thoroughly guilty that we do not. But we have been appallingly un-imaginative in teaching *how* to pray more. So it is with dry duty that we labour at what is intended to be the creative heart of our life and vision. We face the same danger in commending silence.

This section makes practical suggestions for exploring silence in prayer, worship and lifestyle. They are made with the conviction that prayer is the offering of the whole of our being. In the scriptures it finds an incredible range of expression. It involves the physical body, not just the 'soul'. It involves all the senses—of sight, touch, taste, hearing and smell. It involves the whole of life.

It was through the whole of life that God spoke. The 'Word of the Lord' came in a myriad ways. To Jeremiah it came through the blossom on the almond tree (Jer. 1.11) and through watching the potter at work (Jer. 18). For Ezekiel it was a word to taste and eat (Ezek. 3.3)! For Peter it was in a strange dream (Acts 10.9-25).

But not least it was through the offering of the daily routine of life in all its ordinariness to God, that the Word of life would quietly form itself amongst his people.

What we are seeking, in the 'great and ordinary' ways of God, is the quali-ty of quiet attentiveness in all we do, that enables us to receive him as the deepest source of our lives.[2]

A general rule for all these suggestions comes from Dom John Chapman:

  'Pray as you can and do not try to pray as you can't. Take yourself as you find yourself and start from there.'

1. 'Dropping Anchor' (preparing to pray)

A creative use of silence may be the most effective way of stilling our-selves when life is hectic and time is short. it enables us to come before God in gentleness rather than by a violence of will or embattled by 'distractions'.

[1] Mark Medhoff (Amber Lane Press, 1980). A fascinating play revolving around the love of a speech therapist (James) for one of his deaf students (Sarah).

[2] I acknowledge my debt to those guests at Lee Abbey who had joined in workshops on this subject over the year prior to my writing this. Most of the ideas that follow come out of those times of discussion and experiment.

Choose your posture, comfortable but alert. Consider whether a visual focus would be of help—such as a candle, a picture, or a cross. A verse or short passage of scripture is a good anchor to start with.

(a) Breathing: Begin by deepening your breathing slightly into a relaxed natural rhythm. This will help you physically 'wind down' but it also helps your prayer. Let it be so. As you breathe you might silently pray;

'Lord Jesus Christ—have mercy on me'—prayed in and out on the rhythm of your breathing.

or

reflect on 'breath' itself. It is the same word as 'Spirit' in the Bible. God breathed into Adam's nostrils and he became a living being (Gen. 2.7).

or

just relax and let mind and heart lie fallow in God's presence (Ps. 131).

(b) An act of Acceptance: Quietly reflect on the 'world' you have brought with you to prayer—its mood, its problems, its relationships, joys and sorrows. We normally call these 'distractions'. Do not reject them. Gather them up and ask Christ to keep them while you pray. 'Love your enemies' and bring them with you into God's presence.

If 'dropping anchor' is being done as a group it helps to have someone steering the time. It may help to agree the length of silence before you start.

Come out of silence gently. Do not rush into activity. It will have meant different things to each member of the group and there is need to be sensitive. Someone may need a chance to offer a thought for prayer or discussion—God may have spoken in some particular way. But equally, do not be tempted to analyze the silence for the sake of it.

2. Silent Punctuation (Silence and shared worship)
(a) Liturgy: In the liturgies of the Anglican Alternative Service Book there are regular points in the worship where it is suggested that *silence may be kept*. These generally come at points where something has just been received—after the reading of God's Word, after the Eucharistic Prayer and after communion itself. Where congregations grow into the naturalness of such a rhythm there can be a beautiful ebb and flow to the worship without the need to have it all announced. In this way even a noisy family service can have a quality of stillness about it. There is, however, a traditional tendency to fill all gaps in the worship with organ music!

There may be other points at which silence will be appropriate. Jean Vanier once suggested that all Christian celebration should end in silence—to remember those who cannot celebrate.

Above all, if 'a time of silence' is what is intended, make sure it is allowed to be just that! Do you know the poem that begins

'I sat in the church (I'd gone to break bread)
the pastor began to assure us
that we could spend time with our minds fixed on God
—but somebody thought of a chorus!'[1]

(b) Christ in Quiet. A time of quiet meditation may be a helpful alternative to the more formal sermon or even intercession time when we meet as a church. 'Christ in Quiet' is the name given to a daily part of the Lee Abbey programme in the half hour before supper.

It is a mixture of music, readings and silence chosen around a theme and led by a member of the Community. Over the years it has been an enormous help to many people and it is consistently among the most popular features of the programme. But there is no reason why it could not form part of the worship of any congregation.

3. Body and Senses
(a) Movement and Imagination: We have already suggested an example of the use of movement in prayer (see page 16). It can be something explored together or in private prayer. It does not have to be clever—it just needs to be 'you'. There are many times in our lives when we express ourselves more through action than words—why should prayer and worship be any different?

Here are some suggestions for 'action' prayers:
(i)*The Lord's Prayer:* In groups of no more than six people express the Lord's prayer in simple movements. You will need to discuss this but 'keep moving'!

(ii) *Entering God's Courts:* Imagine yourself entering the presence of God as you would be received in a Royal audience. Express this prayer in movement. (This has often been a breakthrough to discover what an aid to prayer the imagination can be—it is traditionally an enemy).

(iii) *In Awe, in Love, in Contrition:* Movement can express our sense of awe and of God's majesty (with Rev. 4.9-11), our love and trust in his goodness (with Ps. 131), our penitence and humbling before him (with Ezek. 1.25ff.).

We might also include at this point the creative actions of writing and drawing. To express your prayer through a poem or drawing can help you explore what the heart of your prayer really is—it disciplines the prayer and gives it content. Once again this is not a question of being 'good at' something. We are simply learning to pray and worship from our true selves.

[1] From 'But somebody thought of a chorus' by Gordon Bailey, *Patchwork Quilt* (SOL Publications, 1975).

(b) The Senses; Another occasional ingredient to a Lee Abbey programme has been something called a 'Silent Walk'. A small group of people will walk together on the estate for half an hour—in complete silence. The intention is to listen and to be sensitive to the world around. They then meet and discuss their impressions. There is always an awareness that the discipline of silence shared had brought a new intensity to the world they walked in. Colours, smells, textures were all received with a new life and vigour. There was always a sense of dismay at how much 'we have been missing' in the normal bustle and wordiness of it all. We neglect our senses to our cost. In silence we can rediscover them. We need hardly add that such a walk will teach us as much about inner cities as countryside.

The senses can find expression in church worship. In some traditions there is much colour and sensitivity of course but it can also become the province of the professionals at the front!

I remember the impact, one Good Friday, of finding a nail provided in the pews. Meditating through touch, on the reality of the cross was a helpful focus. I have also known it done with cups of vinegar! It may be possible to use darkness and light more imaginatively in some churches.

Some church traditions have no place for the nose to worship God! 'Scientists tell us that the nose is the oldest of the organs of our senses and therefore retains an unrivalled power to evoke what is inexpressible' (Laurens Van Der Post). It may take getting used to, but the occasional use of incense in church worship can contribute an important dimension to our expression of God's holiness.

4. Silence in the Diary
There must be 'full stops' in our diaries when we withdraw for a time to be silent. We must not feel guilty of doing so—in fact we will need each other's encouragement to keep it up. It is amazing how easily this commitment drops out of the diary before anything else does!

There may be places nearby that could be a resource in this way—whether for a day or part of a day, or a longer period. Two publications may be of help in exploring this further:

Geoffrey Gerard *Away from it all—A Guide to Retreat Houses* (Lutterworth Press)

Vision (magazine published by the National Retreat Centre, Liddon House, 24 South Audley Street, London W1Y 5DL)

'One Word the Father spoke, which Word was his Son, and this Word he ever speaks in eternal silence and in silence it must be heard by the soul.'

(St. John of the Cross)